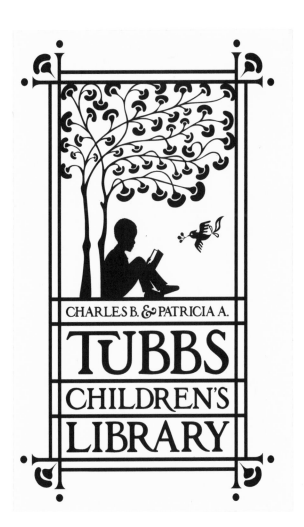

CHARLES B. & PATRICIA A.

TUBBS
CHILDREN'S
LIBRARY

Bugs, Bugs, Bugs!

Cicadas

by Margaret Hall

Consulting Editor: Gail Saunders-Smith, PhD

Consultant: Laura Jesse, Extension Associate
Department of Entomology
Iowa State University
Ames, Iowa

Capstone *press*

Mankato, Minnesota

Pebble Plus is published by Capstone Press,
151 Good Counsel Drive, P.O. Box 669, Mankato, Minnesota 56002.
www.capstonepress.com

1 2 3 4 5 6 11 10 09 08 07 06

Library of Congress Cataloging-in-Publication Data
Hall, Margaret, 1947–
    Cicadas / by Margaret Hall.
    p. cm.—(Bugs, bugs, bugs!)
    Summary: "Simple text and photographs present cicadas, how they look, and what they do"—Provided by publisher.
    Includes bibliographical references and index.
    ISBN-13: 978-0-7368-5349-1 (hardcover)
    ISBN-10: 0-7368-5349-9 (hardcover)
    1. Cicadas—Juvenile literature. I. Title. II. Pebble plus. Bugs, bugs, bugs!
QL527.C5H35 2006
595.7'52—dc22   2005023789

Editorial Credits
Mari C. Schuh, editor; Linda Clavel, set designer; Kia Adams, book designer; Jo Miller, photo researcher; Scott Thoms, photo editor

Photo Credits
Bill Johnson, cover, 13
Corbis/James Leynse, 9
Creatas, back cover
Dennis Manning/Root Resources, 21
Frederick D. Atwood, 7
iStockPhoto/Rhett Stansbury, 1
James P. Rowan, 19
Pete Carmichael, 11
Peter Arnold Inc./J. Brackenbury, 5
Rob Curtis, 17
Visuals Unlimited/Gary Meszaros, 15

Note to Parents and Teachers

The Bugs, Bugs, Bugs! set supports national science standards related to the diversity of life and heredity. This book describes and illustrates cicadas. The images support early readers in understanding the text. The repetition of words and phrases helps early readers learn new words. This book also introduces early readers to subject-specific vocabulary words, which are defined in the Glossary section. Early readers may need assistance to read some words and to use the Table of Contents, Glossary, Read More, Internet Sites, and Index sections of the book.

Table of Contents

What Are Cicadas?

Cicadas are flying insects
with thick bodies.

How Cicadas Look

Some cicadas are
brown or black.
Others are bright colors.

Adult cicadas can be
as long as your little finger.

Cicadas have

long drinking tubes.

Cicadas use their tubes

to suck juice

from trees and plants.

drinking tube

11

Cicadas have
four clear wings
and two large eyes.

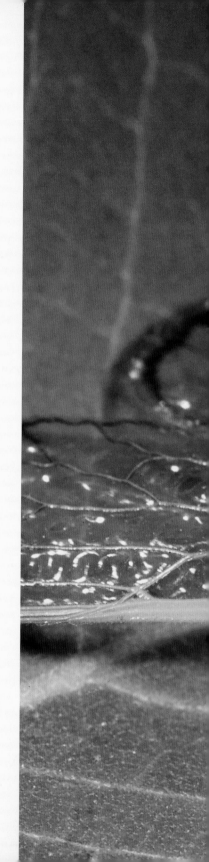

13

What Cicadas Do

Male cicadas make
very loud buzzing noises.
Males buzz to call females.

Male and female cicadas mate.
Females lay eggs in trees.
Nymphs hatch from the eggs
and live underground
for many years.

Nymphs dig out
of the ground.
They shed their skin
as they grow.

Nymphs crawl out of
their skin one last time.
They wait for
their wings to dry.
Now they are adult cicadas.

21

Glossary

drinking tube—a part of the mouth that cicadas use for sucking liquid

female—an animal that can give birth to young animals or lay eggs

hatch—to break out of an egg

insect—a small animal with six legs, three body sections, and two antennas; most insects have wings and can fly.

male—an animal that can be a father

mate—to join together to make young animals

nymph—a young insect that looks like an adult with no wings

shed—to get rid of

Read More

Murray, Peter. *Insects.* Science Around Us. Chanhassen, Minn.: Child's World, 2005.

O'Hare, Ted. *Insects.* What Is an Animal? Vero Beach, Fla.: Rourke, 2006.

Squire, Ann. *Cicadas.* A True Book. New York: Children's Press, 2003.

Internet Sites

FactHound offers a safe, fun way to find Internet sites related to this book. All of the sites on FactHound have been researched by our staff.

Here's how:

1. Visit *www.facthound.com*

2. Type in this special code **0736853499** for age-appropriate sites. Or enter a search word related to this book for a more general search.

3. Click on the **Fetch It** button.

FactHound will fetch the best sites for you!

Index

Word Count: 119
Grade: 1
Early-Intervention Level: 12